GUIDE
FOR VOLUNTEERS

JESUS CENTERED
YOUTH MINISTRY

MOVING FROM JESUS-PLUS TO JESUS-ONLY

Group

RICK LAWRENCE

YouthMinistry.com/TOGETHER

Jesus-Centered Youth Ministry: Guide for Volunteers
Copyright © 2014 Rick Lawrence

group.com
simplyyouthministry.com

Credits
Author: Rick Lawrence
Chief Creative Officer: Joani Schultz
Editor: Rob Cunningham
Copy Editor: Stephanie Martin
Art Director: Veronica Preston
Cover Art: Jeff Storm
Project Manager: Stephanie Krajec

All Scripture quotations, unless otherwise indicated, are taken from the *Holy Bible, New International Version®. NIV®.* Copyright © 1973, 1978, 1984 by International Bible Society. Used by permission of Zondervan. All rights reserved.

Scripture quotations marked NASB are taken from the *New American Standard Bible®.* Copyright © 1960, 1962, 1963, 1968, 1971, 1972, 1973, 1975, 1977, 1995 by The Lockman Foundation. Used by permission. All rights reserved.

Scripture quotations marked THE MESSAGE from ***THE MESSAGE***. Copyright © by Eugene H. Peterson 1993, 1994, 1995, 1996, 2000, 2001, 2002. Used by permission of NavPress Publishing Group.

The website addresses included in this book are offered only as a resource and/or reference for the reader. The inclusion of these websites are not intended, in any way, to be interpreted as an endorsement of these sites or their content on the part of Group Publishing or the author. In addition, the author and Group Publishing do not vouch for the content of these websites for the life of this book.

ISBN 978-1-4707-2073-5
10 9 8 7 6 5 4 3 2 1   20 19 18 17 16 15 14

Printed in the United States of America.

DEDICATION

To the hundreds of thousands of everyday people who work all day at a "normal" job, then give of their precious margin-time to hang out with teenagers—all because you love Jesus and love them. You are my heroes.

CONTENTS

INTRODUCTION

My intent is to help you reorient the way you understand and participate in youth ministry—from a "Jesus-plus" approach to a "Jesus-only" approach. By this I mean moving from a focus that's kinda/sorta about Jesus to one that *breathes* him. And at the beginning, we can't avoid the question that sits like an elephant in our living room:

"What's the big deal about 'Jesus-Centered'—isn't ministry, by definition, already about focusing on Jesus?"

At the core of this little guide to Jesus-centered youth ministry is this truth: We aren't "focusing on Jesus" the way we think we are. People involved in ministry, by and large, have unwittingly and subtly and often forgotten that Jesus is at the center of everything.

It's hard to admit that we've forgotten Jesus in our commonly accepted approaches to ministry and discipleship and Bible study, but the fruits of those conventional practices are drowning out our good intentions. We've unconsciously taken Jesus for granted in the rich excess of Western Christian culture. We've functionally moved on to bigger, better things that seem more relevant to the challenges facing the church: new and innovative church structures, ministry approaches that appeal to postmodern and even post-Christian young people, and social concerns that resonate with globally aware students.

But if a ministry's focus on Jesus is really akin to breathing, then the evidence suggests that most churches, and most youth ministries, are using a ventilator to stay alive. They don't *breathe Jesus* with the force of their own passionate impetus. We'll explore the truth about this impossible reality from many vantage points, because the impossible has happened in the Western church. But more importantly, we'll discover together what a *Jesus-centered ministry* actually looks and sounds and tastes like.

BORED BY EVERYTHING BUT JESUS

A decade ago, I was invited to speak at a youth ministry conference hosted by a very large church in the Midwest. The organizers asked me to lead a two-hour pre-conference session for youth workers who wanted something a little deeper, a little more revolutionary. At the time, I was experimenting with a training idea that focused every aspect of youth ministry on a deepening attachment to Jesus. As we explored the possibilities together, a subtle shift of atmosphere grew in the room. By the end of those two hours, that little gathering of 30 or so youth workers had become a runaway worship-train. We were crying and laughing and hungry for more of Jesus. At the end, some people in the room with many long years of ministry on their résumé waited in line to tell me a sobering revelation: that they'd never really tasted deeply of Jesus and had never appreciated his height and depth and breadth. I understood exactly what they were trying to say.

So when I emerged from that two-hour training session that had morphed into something much bigger and better, my appetite for Jesus was voracious. And with my leadership responsibilities completed, I was free to roam the rest of the conference, popping into as many workshops and general sessions as I could cram in. I listened to many of the best experts in youth ministry that day, all of them brilliant and many of them longtime friends. But by the end of the day, I felt a growing restlessness—a reaction to a *deadening* in my soul as I tried to process the onslaught of ministry "tips and techniques."

As evening settled in, that deadness had spread into a kind of depression, so I found an empty, overstuffed chair in the huge and bustling atrium. I needed to pray, and it was easy to isolate myself in the middle of the throng. In my "cone of silence," I asked a simple question: "Why, why, why, Jesus, am I feeling this way?" Tears streamed down my face, and pain was in my eyes. And then, in one of those moments when the voice of Jesus is crystal clear, he said this to me:

"You're bored by everything but me now."

I knew it was true as soon as I heard it. Great strategies and tested principles for ministry are fine; they just can't replace the intoxicating presence of Jesus. If you showed up at a cooking class and discovered Oprah was teaching it, you'd probably be less impressed with her recipes and more interested in...*her*. I'd always defined discipleship as a progression that looked a lot like doing well in school—studying hard, growing in knowledge, doing well on "tests." But those things, I realized, now paled in comparison to the undeniable truth: True disciples are captured and carried away by Jesus. They are so "stuck" on him that the natural outcome of their attachment to him is a perpetual willingness to give over their life to him. They are ruined by Jesus and ruined for Jesus.

When Jesus is the center of everything, and when people are drawn into closer orbit around him, fruit happens. That's just the way things work. The rest of this book serves as a welcome mat into a whole new reality. Walk through this door and you'll discover a new way of leading and loving students that feels simpler and more purposeful. And along the way, you'll find what your soul has always craved.

CHAPTER ONE

Problem?
What Problem?

"Holy Bat-Signal, Batman!" —Robin

The central question of the book the WWJD frenzy was based on, Charles Sheldon's *In His Steps*,[1] is simple: "If Christians are supposed to be following Jesus, why aren't they making more of an impact in their daily lives?" The book's answer was to imagine what everyday life might be like if all of us simply talked and acted more like Jesus. Well, that *would* change everything, but as far as I could tell during the 1990s from my perch as editor of Group Magazine, the What Would Jesus Do movement *hadn't* changed everything.

There are two inherent problems at the core of WWJD:

1. Our guesses about what Jesus *would do* in our contemporary circumstances are directly tied to how well we know and understand *what he's already done*, and our record there is pretty bad.

2. Jesus was fundamentally unpredictable—he's the most surprising person you'll ever know. It's hard to predict what surprising people *will do*, but that doesn't mean it's hard to *know their heart*.

ROMANCE VS. ROTE

People who are caught up in a romantic relationship don't have to be told to focus on their beloved; it's hard to stop thinking about the person, actually. No matter what we're doing or who we're with, our thoughts stray to the object of our passion. To use the language of C.H. Spurgeon (more on him later), our life is "beelined" to our beloved. But it isn't the momentum of a "should"—it's the attraction of a lover. There's an enormous distinction between the two.

Teenagers today are staying away from church—or leaving it altogether—because so many of them have been "shoulded" into a relationship with God or the church. If they, instead, had a kind of romantic attachment to Jesus—a passion for him that created a beeline momentum in their life—they'd not only stay connected to the church, they'd also bring a bunch of their friends with them.

The body of Christ in Western culture is facing an emergency. More than 200,000 churches in the United States are in decline. Every year, more than 4,000 of them close their doors for good. The people who've stuck with the church have a higher average age than the general population, and if you backtrack through the generations you'll find that the younger people are, the less likely they are to be connected with a church.

Of course, the United States continues to be a "Christian nation," with 95 percent of Americans believing in God. But the most generous estimate of the percentage of people who still attend church regularly is 40 percent, and the real weekly attendance figure is almost certainly closer to 17 percent (the number pegged by researchers who actually count Sunday attenders). And here's the real kick in the gut: In the space of just five years, the percentage of teenagers attending church every week has plummeted by 25 percent (from 20 percent to 15 percent).[2]

All our conventional responses to this steamrolling crisis have missed the mark. We've tried to become more relevant, more glitzy, more tolerant, more technologically savvy, more flexible, more professional, more sophisticated, more purpose-driven, more comprehensive, more socially aware, more...more. But all our "mores" have done nothing to reverse the trend of disengagement.

THE DISAPPEARING JESUS

I was talking with a junior high girl who'd just served as a leader in a churchwide worship experience during Holy Week. She'd spent several days leading people from her congregation into a deeper relationship with Jesus through an interactive devotional experience. The girl was giddy with excitement about the whole thing. I told her I like to ask teenagers to describe Jesus to me—just because I'm curious about how they see him.

"So," I asked, "what are some words you'd use to describe Jesus to someone who's never heard of him?"

She scrunched her forehead and tried to wrestle that question to the ground. Finally, she offered this hopeful response: "Well, I'd have to say he's really, really nice."

She was ready to leave it right there, so I asked: "Remember that time Jesus made a whip and chased all the money changers out of the Temple? Does that story change the way you'd describe Jesus?"

She scrunched her forehead again. The smile disappeared from her face. I'd created a kind of intolerable dissonance in her. Finally, with a tone of desperation, she landed on this: "Well, I know Jesus is nice, so what he did must have been nice." I nodded politely and thanked her for thinking through her response.

Soon after, I launched a Group Magazine project—we hired video crews in five major metropolitan areas to stop teenagers randomly on the street and ask them a simple question: "How would you describe Jesus?" When I got all the raw footage back, I quickly discovered my experience with the junior high girl wasn't an aberration.

Without fail, teenagers' first and favorite descriptive word for Jesus was always *nice*.[3]

And this reality was profoundly sad for me. Sure, Jesus was "nice" to the people he healed or fed or rescued. But he would never be voted Mr. Congeniality. He definitely wasn't nice when he was blasting (over and over) religious leaders or calling his lead disciple "Satan" or a persistent Canaanite woman a "dog" or telling the rich young ruler to sell all his possessions and follow him if that ruler wanted to "inherit eternal life." In Matthew 23, in The Message paraphrase, Jesus told the Pharisees they were "hopeless"—not once, but *seven times* in a row—and then he planted three exclamation marks at the end of that diatribe, calling them "manicured grave plots," "total frauds," and "snakes."

The point is that a *merely* nice Jesus is no Jesus at all. And if Jesus isn't really Jesus to you, your connection to the church will devolve into a fragile cultural commitment, not a real relationship with a real person. My pastor, Tom Melton, once told me: "We don't really believe Jesus is beautiful; otherwise, we wouldn't describe our relationship with him as so much work." We "work at" our relationship with Jesus, and urge our teenagers to do the same, because the nicey-nice Jesus we've settled for *requires us to work* if we want to maintain a connection to him, or worship him, or serve him. The false Jesus of our conventional narratives arouses no passion in students.

Their passivity toward him is a natural result of the milquetoast descriptions they've heard of him.

Nicey-nice Jesus isn't strong and fierce and *big* enough to walk with students (or us) into the fiery furnaces of everyday life. Teenagers are facing big challenges and struggles, and they're looking for someone or something to help them through or give them the courage they need to survive the blows they've endured. Because the only Jesus young people have experienced in the church is a Mr. Rogers knockoff, they've naturally turned to "lesser gods" that promise better results, including:

- humanism

- social justice

- drugs and alcohol

- affluence

- video games

- social networking

- sexual experimentation

- spirituality

- sports

- academic achievement

Today's teenagers just aren't getting who Jesus really is, or they aren't getting *enough* of who he really is, or they're getting, literally, a fake Jesus. As a result, few of them are living passionately with Christ in their everyday lives. According to Dr. Christian Smith's research for the National Study of Youth and Religion (youthandreligion.org), 9 out of 10 American young people (and their parents) don't have what social researchers call a "devoted" faith. That means:

- their faith in Christ isn't central to their life;

- they don't know the basics of their faith (our own research finds that 4 out of 10 of Christian teenagers say "a good person can earn eternal salvation through good deeds," and almost a quarter of them say Jesus "committed sins while he lived on earth"); and

- they don't see Jesus making an impact in their everyday life—he's merely a church thing.[4]

THE ONSET OF APATHY

Without the passion of a "devoted faith" in Jesus, all that's left is a cultural commitment to churchgoing. And we all know *that* cultural norm is quickly evaporating.

An "off the radar" church that is overshadowed by a growing secularization in our culture means that an "all-in" relationship with Jesus is far down the list of teenagers' priorities. Instead, the National Study of Youth and Religion found that kids essentially see God as a "divine butler" or a "cosmic therapist." Jesus' job is to be all-in with their needs and their problems, while making no demands on their time, their talents, or their passions. He exists to help them do what they want, to make them happy, and to solve their problems.

The hard truth is that this entrenched attitude is the natural byproduct of the church environment teenagers have been exposed to. Our research pegs the number of kids who say they've learned "Jesus is God" at church at an overwhelming 87 percent.[5] But that's a semantic panacea. The truth is that too few of them are getting a healthy exposure to the barefaced Jesus of the Bible, and too many of them have heard what *we think* about Jesus. But they're not experiencing his raw presence for themselves. According to the NSYR, most American young people believe that:

- God exists, and this being created and orders the world and watches over human life on earth.

- This God wants people to be good, nice, and fair to each other—as taught in the Bible and by most world religions.

- The central goal of life is to be happy and to feel good about yourself.

- God doesn't need to be particularly involved in your life, except when you need him to resolve a problem.

- Good people go to heaven when they die.

- Church is just another thing on a to-do list; it isn't a context where they enjoy their closest friendships.

This list of functional beliefs offers no evidence that young people have a ruined-for-Jesus perspective on life. For almost all teenagers, Jesus isn't the hub of their life. They have no firm idea of who Jesus really is, why he came, what he actually said, what he actually did, or what he's doing now. And when something happens in their "real" world, they struggle to understand how Jesus is a part of it.

Many likely reasons exist for this crisis of discipleship in the church, but they aren't THE REASON. This is it:

Life is draining out of the Western church—and most youth ministries—because we're not setting the kind of growth environment that is conducive for disciples.

CHAPTER TWO

Be the Pig

"Christ be with me, Christ within me. Christ behind me, Christ before me. Christ beside me, Christ to win me. Christ to comfort and restore me. Christ beneath me, Christ above me. Christ in quiet, Christ in danger. Christ in hearts of all that love me. Christ in mouth of friend and stranger."
—St. Patrick

Our challenge is to make the pursuit of Jesus the central, consuming, desperate focus of our ministry with teenagers. The French Laundry in Napa Valley is one of the world's top-rated restaurants. If you work there, the highest honor you can receive is a T-shirt given by the owner to a select few. The T-shirt slogan "Be the Pig" refers to the difference between pigs and chickens. A chicken might offer up an egg for the meal, but the pig gives his life for it. All-in disciples of Jesus are pigs, not chickens.

The clearest biblical translation of this kind of "be the pig" discipleship is described in John 6. It happened 2,000 years ago on a lonely Capernaum beachfront. When the massive crowds following the rock-star Jesus—those who've been captured by his miracles, healings, and teachings—hear him say, seven times in a row, that they must "eat the flesh of the Son of Man and drink his blood" or they'll have "no life in yourselves," they're disgusted and disoriented enough to escape him en masse. And after the dust and noise from their retreat has cleared, Jesus looks at his remaining 12 disciples— also likely disgusted and disoriented—and asks this incredible question: "You do not want to leave, too, do you?" And, here, Peter steps to the plate and answers like a pig, so to speak: "Lord, to whom shall we go? You have words of eternal life. We believe and know that you are the Holy One of God."

Peter, like the masses who've just stampeded down the hill, scrambling to get away from Jesus, would likely escape him if he could. But he just can't. He so identifies himself with Jesus that he can't imagine leaving him. Peter is all-in, a pig not a chicken, and this is what discipleship *really* looks like. Later Paul, another all-in disciple—one of the greatest thinkers and apologists in history—describes his orientation to Jesus this way: "I resolved to know nothing while I was with you except Jesus Christ and him crucified" (1 Corinthians 2:2).

I believe youth ministries, and churches in general, have been using a flawed strategy for discipleship that produces chickens, not pigs. I call it the "understand and apply" strategy. It assumes people grow deeper in their faith when they understand biblical principles and apply them to their lives. "Understand and apply" has proven to be a marginal strategy, at best, and has weak biblical support. The ultimate reason teenagers stop following Christ after high school is that *they can*—they're not "ruined" for him, as Peter was when Jesus asked if he was going to leave, too. A disciple's answer to that question is something like: "I don't understand a lot of what you're saying, and I can't comprehend the things you do, but I know I have nowhere else to go. You've ruined me for you." Disciples answer this way because of the depth of their attachment to Jesus.

Because of the vast number of other environmental forces that are shaping teenagers today, *only* a deeper attachment to Jesus has any chance of stopping the church's slide toward the abyss. But we can't "should" teenagers into an all-in relationship with Jesus, any more than I "shoulded" my wife into marrying me. For true intimacy to grow in any relationship, we have to be captured and consumed by our lover's *essence*. Pastor and theologian N.T. Wright says: "The longer you look at Jesus, the more you will want to serve him. That is, of course, if it's the real Jesus you're looking at."[6] It's "the real Jesus" whose gravitational pull is so strong that we can't escape his orbit once we get close to him. Philosophy professor and C.S. Lewis scholar Dr. Peter Kreeft once told a class of Boston University students:

> "Christ changed every human being he ever met. ... If anyone claims to have met him without being changed, he has not met him at all. When you touch him, you touch lightning. ... I think Jesus is the only man in history who never bored anyone. I think this is an empirical fact, not just a truth of faith. It's one of the reasons for believing his central claim, and Christianity's central claim, that he is literally God in the flesh. ... The Greek word used to describe everyone's reaction to him

in the Gospels is thauma—*wonder. This was true of his enemies, who killed him. Of his disciples, who worshipped him. And even of agnostics, who went away shaking their heads and muttering 'No man every spoke like this man' and knowing that if he didn't stop being what he was and saying what he said that eventually they would have to side with either his killers or his worshippers. For 'Jesus-shock' breaks your heart in two and forces you to choose which half of your heart you will follow."*[7]

In our conventional understand-and-apply mentality, our central role is to answer kids' questions and "should" them toward better choices in their life. But if we see our primary role as answering questions and *shoulding*, that job description quickly becomes impossible. Urban youth ministry expert Leneita Fix gave me this sampler of questions, asked one night by her small group of senior highers:

How do I know if someone is demon-possessed?

Why doesn't my Jewish friend believe Jesus is the Messiah?

Don't Jewish people believe Abraham is Satan?

In those paranormal-type movies, are ghosts and demons the same thing?

Why don't we ever get to stop sinning?

Why does my Jehovah's Witness friend make me feel like I'm the one who's wrong?

Good luck with those, Leneita. When we accept our "answer-person" job description, we back ourselves into the corner of incapacity sooner or later. All of us will get crammed into that corner because "the right answers" have replaced "the right orientation," and it's literally impossible for any human being to respond well to the myriad environmental forces that are leveraging our teenagers. Frustration is a foregone conclusion, *because we don't have all the answers*, and we have a pretty miserable record of teaching people to "apply" truths. Real transformation, even in our own experience, most often happens differently than "understand and apply."

In a Group Magazine survey, we asked Christian college students to look back over their trajectory and identify the factors that caused them to grow and mature as followers of Christ. They told us their primary catalysts included:

1. Parents

2. A crisis or a great struggle

3. A camp or retreat experience

The common thread among these influences is that they're all *identity-forming* forces rather than *understand-and-apply* forces. In contrast to relational experiences that shape our identity in Christ, the understand-and-apply heresy promotes two glaring fallacies:

1. "Understand and apply" assumes that mere understanding leads to growth. If understanding alone were a true indicator of growth as a disciple, then Satan should step to the head of the class. He knew enough biblical truth to go toe-to-toe with Jesus in the wilderness. Understanding alone, it's obvious, does not guarantee transformation. The road to Emmaus demonstrates that, for at least two of Jesus' disciples, much of what the Good Shepherd tried to get across to his sheep hadn't really "stuck." They'd heard him, lived with him, and watched him, but they hadn't yet been transformed by him. One crucial step was left: to move from an *outside* influence to an *inside* influence. And that's why the Holy Spirit is so necessary. The Spirit makes it possible for us to move from *knowing about* Jesus to *knowing* Jesus. This is *knowing* in the "biblical sense"—it's our most intimate act.

2. "Understand and apply" assumes that our growth in Christ is dependent on our ability, or willingness, to apply truth to our lives. When you're sitting in church, count the number of times some version of "apply this to your life" is mentioned. Then ask yourself:

"What's the likelihood that most people sitting in this room will leave here and immediately begin applying these truths to their lives?" Or even more telling: "What's the likelihood that most people in this room even *understand* how to apply the truths they just heard or have the willpower to consider applying them?" The sheep don't need a better understanding of how to avoid getting eaten by wolves; they need a deeper trust in and obedience to their Shepherd, who will look out for them, defend them, and rescue them.

A RADICAL CHANGE IN FOCUS

In his book *Ruthless Trust*, author Brennan Manning wrote: "It must be noted that Jesus alone reveals who God is. ... We cannot deduce anything about Jesus from what we think we know about God; however, we must deduce everything about God from what we know about Jesus."[8] The imperative lurking in Manning's blast of truth is an eccentric, ultra-curious, passionate pursuit of everything Jesus said and did. We learn "everything about God" from paying much, much closer attention to Jesus than we ever have before. And when we do, we'll rediscover the original path to a transformed life, laid out by the Trinity from the dawn of time: "Eat my body, drink my blood."

The movement from "mastering knowledge" and growing students' impetus to act on that knowledge, to something that looks and sounds more like a growing romance that "ruins" the lover for the Beloved is at the core of the Jesus-centered ministry shift. And to make this shift, we'll need to do something that couples who've been married a long time and have grown dull to one another's beauty must do: We must remember the Jesus we didn't know we'd forgotten.

Remembering is central to God's movement in our lives. That means *forgetting* is our greatest enemy. We're way, way too comfortable and satisfied in our knowledge and understanding and experience of Jesus. Our forgetting is caused by a sense that we have everything under control ourselves. And the more *on top of things* the sheep think they are, the more exposed they are to danger, because they'll be less interested in listening to and obeying their Shepherd and more committed to fighting their own (impossible-to-win) battles.

Paul, in his old age and with the end of his life on the horizon, gave his protégé Timothy this bit of parting advice: "*Remember* Jesus Christ, raised from the dead, descended from David. This is my gospel, for which I am suffering even to the point of being chained like a criminal" (2 Timothy 2:8-9, emphasis added). Paul was imprisoned because of his aggressive pursuit of Jesus, and Timothy had lived through beatings and shipwrecks and imprisonments with him—all for the glory and honor of Jesus. Why would Paul have to *remind* Timothy about Jesus? He was humble enough to admit the truth: Everyone, including Paul, Timothy, John the Baptist, Peter, and the disciples...and now you and me...is a notorious forgetter.

When Group Magazine asked more than 25,000 Christian teenagers what topic they were most interested in talking about with their youth leader or other adult ministry leader, their top response was this: "Getting a better understanding of what Jesus really said and did, and how faith in him matters in my own life."

JESUS AND HIS BOTANICAL BENT

God's "love language" is metaphor. And Jesus defined discipleship and growth using metaphors, most often in botanical terms: "I am the Vine, you are the branches. When you're joined with me and I with you, the relation intimate and organic, the harvest is sure to be abundant. Separated, you can't produce a thing" (John 15:5-6, THE MESSAGE). Later, Paul builds on the foundation of Jesus' metaphor by extending its meaning: "If some of the branches have been broken off, and you, though a wild olive shoot, have been grafted in among the others and now share in the nourishing sap from the olive root, do not boast over those branches. If you do, consider this: You do not support the root, but the root supports you" (Romans 11:17-18).

This grafted-into-the-Vine metaphor is telling us a kingdom-of-God truth—that we're dying branches in desperate need of attaching ourselves to a growing Vine, and the Vine is Jesus himself. The truth is that transformation happens when we attach ourselves more deeply to Jesus, because he's the only one who can really change us. My friend Ned Erickson once shared with me something he calls "The Progression." It goes like this: "Get to know Jesus well, because the more you know him, the more you'll love him, and the more you love him, the more you'll want to follow him, and the more you follow him, the more you'll become like him, and the more you become like him, the more you become yourself."[9] A "self" that is fully alive, and fully itself, is the organic outcome of a deepening attachment to the Vine. And it's the organic outcome that Jesus is after, not "try harder to get better."

When we move from a ministry focus that emphasizes knowledge alone to an environment that helps students experience Jesus, we are helping their graft to "take." And once they are grafted to Jesus, their identity is caught up in him. They, like Peter, will move into their lives as true disciples who answer, "Where else would I go?" when they're offered the chance to leave him. And fruit will fill up their lives, offering others the nourishment they so desperately need.

ANSWERING THE ONLY TWO QUESTIONS THAT MATTER

Though this shift to a Jesus-centered passion and approach sounds big—and it is—the steps onto this path are remarkably simple. I don't mean this will be like flipping on a light switch; I mean that our ministry focus can now be reduced to helping students pursue the answers to two simple questions:

1. **"Who do I say Jesus is?"** After another tough encounter with the conniving Pharisees, followed by another head-scratching conversation with his confused and clueless disciples, Jesus does something that is shocking for its humility. Matthew, the former tax collector on the take, offers this eyewitness account: "Now when Jesus came into the district of Caesarea Philippi, He was asking His disciples, 'Who do people say that the Son of Man is?' And they said, 'Some *say* John the Baptist; and others, Elijah; but still others, Jeremiah, or one of the prophets.' He said to them, 'But who do you say that I am?' Simon Peter answered, 'You are the Christ, the Son of the living God' " (Matthew 16:13-15, NASB).

2. **"Who does Jesus say I am?"** Of course Peter steps up and answers Jesus with magnificent chutzpah. He, more than any other, is attached to Jesus. But attachment is a two-way street; we name Jesus, and Jesus names us.

So Jesus fires back with his own chutzpah: "You are Peter, and upon this rock I will build My church; and the gates of Hades will not overpower it. I will give you the keys of the kingdom of heaven; and whatever you bind on earth shall have been bound in heaven, and whatever you loose on earth shall have been loosed in heaven" (Matthew 16:18-19, NASB).

We name, and are named ourselves, as we beeline our life to Jesus. Our purpose in life narrows in focus, simply, to feeding our fascination of everything he said or did, then moving through life responding to the Spirit's nudges and imperatives. We move Jesus from the background of our everyday activities into the foreground. We are released into our name (our beautiful and unique and desperately needed strength) when we attach ourselves to Jesus so deeply that we can stand and name him when it costs us to do it. And when we orbit everything we do in ministry around answering those two great questions—"Who do I say Jesus is?" and "Who does Jesus say I am?"—we create a kind of *gravitational pull* that magnetically draws (or sometimes repels) students and adults.

CHAPTER
THREE

The Beeline
Practices

The shift to a two-question Jesus-centered youth ministry will mean that everything you do revolves around the pursuit of these questions ("Who do I say Jesus is?" and "Who does Jesus say I am?"). To make these two questions the focus, you'll need to shift away from "talking at" teenagers to asking lots more questions that encourage them to pursue Jesus. Later in this book, we'll explore how to embrace and live out a way of living and engaging others that will create an orbital center around the pursuit of Jesus. As this way of living and leading becomes the norm, the gravitational pull you've created around Jesus will grow stronger and stronger. Plus, as kids get closer and closer to Jesus, the fruit will start flying off of them.

Of course, not all of these practices will fit your ministry or your particular leadership style, but most will...

1. Beeline the Bible—The 19th-century British pastor and theologian C. H. Spurgeon was scorned by the "Pharisees" of his time—they accused him of pandering to the "proletariat" by oversimplifying the Christian life. But one man's oversimplifying is another man's prophetic vision. Spurgeon was, indeed, an advocate of a life and a ministry that's stripped down to its high-performance Ferrari engine: "A sermon without Christ as its beginning, middle, and end is a mistake in conception and a crime in execution."[10] Spurgeon's beelined-to-Jesus focus transcends flash-in-the-pan ministry trends and experiments.

So to create a Jesus-centered environment for youth ministry, we'll need to start by beelining the Bible. Instead of approaching Bible study or Bible teaching from a life-application angle, we use interesting topics—and every Bible passage—as the first step on a path toward Jesus. No matter where we're studying in the Bible, or what topic we're studying, we always—*always*—find a beeline to Jesus.

As I train youth workers to beeline the Bible in their ministries, I ask one person in a small group to close their eyes, open a Bible, and pick a random passage. Then, together with others in their group, the blind Bible-stabber has just five minutes to identify the beeline to Christ from the random passage and brainstorm a plan to teach that passage in a Jesus-centered way. No matter what the passage, the idea is to put that passage in the context of Jesus' life and ministry.

It's good to remember that John's Gospel tells us Jesus is "the Word"—Jesus' fingerprints are all over the Bible. There's a built-in beeline to Jesus no matter where you go in Scripture. And it's our imperative (and our grand adventure) to find it. Simply put, our challenge is to never again teach from the Bible, or plan a Bible study, or launch into a topical study of any kind, without making a beeline to Jesus. Never again.

Let me show you how this works when I choose a random passage in the Bible:

First, I close my eyes, and then I stab my finger into my Bible and come up with Job 5:22. It's in the middle of a speech by Eliphaz (one of Job's "friends") titled "The Innocent Do Not Suffer." The "advice" that encompasses verse 22 (where I've added emphasis) actually starts in verse 17:

"Blessed is the man whom God corrects; so do not despise the discipline of the Almighty. For he wounds, but he also binds up; he injures, but his hands also heal. From six calamities he will rescue you; in seven no harm will befall you. In famine he will ransom you from death, and in battle from the stroke of the sword. You will be protected from the lash of the tongue, and need not fear when destruction comes. *You will laugh at destruction and famine, and need not fear the beasts of the earth.*"

So I close my eyes again and pray: *Jesus, where is the beeline to you?* In a moment, I have it (I'm sure there are many more ways to go with this, but this is the one that surfaces for me in this moment): "What does Jesus *really* promise us?" I'd compare Eliphaz's view of a God who punishes the bad and rewards the good to Jesus' mission to love even his enemies. And I'd scan the Gospels to pluck out every promise Jesus made and compare them to what Eliphaz *represents* as God's promises. That's the beeline.

I've trained thousands of youth pastors to do what I just did. And it's normally a lot easier to do than the experiment I just shared with you, because we're not choosing random Scripture passages when we teach or study. The effect of finding the beeline every time we crack open the Bible (or tap on our Bible app) is that we sink into the truth Spurgeon discovered: that all roads lead to the metropolis of Christ. It will change forever the way students view Scripture study, mission trips, service projects, games, retreats, and, most importantly, their everyday lives.

2. Create Dependent Experiences—Timothy Keller says: "Teenagers have more information about God than they have experiences of him. Get them in places where they have to rely on God."[11] Here's a great example of how one Colorado youth pastor, Josh Jones, lived out this imperative. A couple of summers ago he decided it was time to lurch his ministry out of its mission-trip rut. Every year they'd load up their 12-passenger van and head south for the 28-hour trek to Mexico and a weeklong work camp. And every year, as they traveled through countless towns and cities on the way to their mission focus, they saw dozens of ministry opportunities they were forced to pass by. Those "on the way" possibilities planted the seed of an idea in Josh and his teenagers. So on the heels of a semester-long teaching series that focused on a dependent relationship with the Holy Spirit, Josh gathered his students for something he called "The Magical Mystery Tour."

Essentially, Josh told his students and their parents that during the week they'd normally travel to Mexico, they'd be following the Holy Spirit's leading instead and go on this Magical Mystery Tour. They'd have no planned destination, and no planned service opportunities. Instead, they committed to praying through their days, and staying close to Jesus, then acting on "nudges" to respond to needs they encountered along the way. They started by meeting early in the morning in the church parking lot, where they'd spread a map of the state on the ground. One of the girls tossed a few pebbles over her shoulder, and most of them landed near a town in Western Colorado. So they got in their van and headed out. By the end of that week they'd helped dozens of people in towns and byways along their path, and they'd had an unforgettable experience in what it feels like to depend upon Jesus.

That weeklong experiment in Spirit-dependence is a super-charged example of an everyday practice that reorients our lives from self-reliance to Jesus-attachment. Dependent experiences like the Magical Mystery Tour shove teenagers into a viscerally reliant relationship with Jesus, and that radically deepens their attachment to him. That's why dependent experiences are at the heart of a Jesus-centered ministry. Researchers with the Exemplary Youth Ministry project discovered that the 21 "exemplary" youth ministries they identified in the United States have made an art form out of inviting their students to depend on Jesus. They put their kids in the "hot seat" of ministry leadership and participation, rather than the "cold seat" of ministry consumption. Here are some examples.

- Johnny Derouen, former youth pastor at Travis Avenue Baptist Church in Fort Worth, Texas, says: "My job is to teach the students and adults and parents...how to do ministry. I give it back to them, and it is their ministry. ... The high school students are trained at school to do things by themselves, and I'm not going to do it for them when they get here. The whole program is geared to push you to the next level. ... By the time you are a junior or senior you are leading the program, you're leading small groups, mission-trip groups, you're running the programs. You don't have to, but it is expected—it leads to maturity."

- An adult volunteer at New Colony Baptist Church in Billerica, Massachusetts, says: "The kids take such ownership. They plan and help with the worship and then lead the rest of the group. They've made songs, a movie. We're doing an experience tomorrow—it's not us standing in front of them telling them what to say and what to do."

- A teenage girl at Newport Mesa Christian Center in Costa Mesa, California, once wrote, as a joke, that she'd like to play cowbell during the worship time. "I was totally kidding. But next week Lynette [the youth pastor] gave me a cowbell and I was playing during worship. I didn't even know how to play. If you want to lead clapping during worship, they will make a place for you."

The practice of creating dependent experiences for students simply means we find ways to place ourselves, and students, in God-dependent situations. That means we must risk the pristine results we're sure our own efforts will produce and opt for the messy unknown of teenagers learning how to trust Jesus and experiment their way into the unknown. Simply, we're nudged toward dependence on God when we're placed in dependent circumstances.

And one simple way to move kids from independence to dependence is to change the way we teach them to pray. A.W. Tozer once said: "If you do all the talking when you pray, how will you ever hear God's answers?" So instead of simply "brainstorming" our prayers, we stop first and pause in silence to ask Jesus to guide us. It's a simple "How should I pray, Jesus?" Then we wait, then we pray accordingly. Such dependent prayer is almost unheard of in the church. The more we model dependent prayer for our students, the closer they will get to Jesus. Listen first, then pray.

3. Tell the Truth About Jesus—Kids typically describe Jesus in ways that have little relationship to what he *really* said and did. They think he's a nice, good man—kind of a Barney for grown-ups. He isn't the Jesus of the Bible, or even the Jesus of C.S. Lewis' *Chronicles of Narnia*, where he's retranslated into King Aslan, a ferocious-for-good lion who looms over all seven fantasy stories.

Yes, Jesus was a "nice guy" when he healed people or fed them miraculously or saved them from certain death or demon possession. But he was also so fierce with hypocritical religious leaders and used such profane language to describe them that they conspired to execute him. The Jesus of the Bible is more dangerous than nice; actually, he's more *everything* than the way he's typically described.

We have unwittingly contributed to kids' wrong impressions of Jesus by filtering the Bible's descriptions of what he said and did through our own skewed assumptions. If we, instead, simply allowed the biblical account of his personality and behavior to be our unfiltered instructor, we would find (and teach about) a Jesus who shatters our sensibilities. G.K. Chesterton once said: "If you meet the Jesus of the Gospels, you must redefine what love is, or you won't be able to stand him." This is so deeply true. Jesus was a difficult person; a lot of people were uncomfortable in his presence and were scandalized by things he said and did. It's hard to "stand"

Jesus if you're really paying attention to what he did and said. He is the most redemptively disruptive person who ever walked the earth. He is so much better than our typical descriptions of him, and so much more than a dispenser of life lessons or a teller of pithy fables.

Vintage Church in North Carolina decided to satirize the "fake Jesus" most young people have come to know—to chip away at their wrong notions of Jesus so they could be reintroduced to him. They repurposed a campy old film about Jesus by extracting four scenes from it and then recording their own dialogue to replace the original audio. The result is hilarious (you can check out the videos on YouTube by searching for "Vintage Church Jesus Videos"). They gave Jesus a falsetto Mr. Rogers voice, making him the "nice," pansy Jesus so many kids imagine anyway. Then they cleverly morphed Jesus into a distant rule-keeper who's out of touch with real life and not at all interested in an intimate relationship.

These video parodies are brilliant because they use humor to expose the false, ridiculous Jesus that teenagers often think is the true Jesus. Vintage Church understood that students would never trust this popular-but-fake Jesus with what really matters to them. Here's how to fuel a similar momentum in a youth ministry...

- **First we deconstruct (literally tear apart) the false Jesus that's been embedded in**

students' hearts and minds. We do this by unearthing and confronting fallacies about him as a regular ministry practice. It's as simple as slowing down to ask our standard what/when/where/why/how questions: "What did Jesus really say/do here?" "When did he say/do it?" "Where did this all happen?" "Why did he say/do this?" "How did he say/do this?" As we question, we're digging for the truth about Jesus. We don't accept knee-jerk responses or "Christianese." We're determined to get to the bottom of Jesus, so to speak. Our goal is to move students from patterns of lazy thinking to active engagement.

- **Then we reconstruct and reintroduce the biblical Jesus to students, tying everything we do back into the pursuit of him—using Spurgeon's beeline as our determined strategy.** It's an easy bridge from questioning fallacies about Jesus to embracing Chesterton's challenge to "meet the Jesus of the Gospels." This will require that we redefine what love is because Jesus never did anything outside of love. We'll have to look Jesus full in the face and not shy away from the things he did that make us uncomfortable, confused, or even angry. I call this "standing in mud puddles," because there are so many stories about Jesus that are difficult to understand, so we simply jump over them as if they were mud puddles. The way to get to know Jesus better is to stand in those mud puddles—continue to focus on them until we have some understanding of why Jesus said or did certain things.

4. Focus on the Red Stuff—We who are in ministry are often home-blind.

Home-blind people have lost their sense of the "otherness" of Jesus. We've become so acclimated to the cultural framework we've built around him and the conventional ways we understand him that he becomes functionally invisible. The effect is that we unconsciously push people away from him. We've spent so many years "dialing in" what we believe about Jesus that we fight against evidence that contradicts our assumptions.

It's time to stir up the "sleeping giant" inside our own soul and shake ourselves awake to our own blindness. One profound way we can regain our sight is by focusing on the red stuff. When I was a kid, every Bible printed the words of Jesus in red. It's a little less common today but still a popular practice. Red means "pay attention." Of course, all of the Bible is important to study, but the words of Jesus invite special attention because the Bible's whole narrative points to him. In a Jesus-centered youth ministry, the "red stuff" of the Bible is a staple in every context. Simply, it means we give greater focus to the things Jesus actually said.

My favorite way to focus on the red stuff is to ask the "Oprah Question." Near the back of every O Magazine, Oprah asks her celebrity guests this brilliant question: "What's one thing you know for sure?" I've co-opted this question and extended it to this: "Based on this Scripture passage, what's one thing you know for sure about Jesus?" I'll demonstrate how this works in a moment, but first it's important to emphasize how this simple question can operate like a redemptive (red) stop sign in so many ministry arenas, not just for portions of Scripture that include Jesus' words. You can also ask the modified Oprah Question ("What do you know for sure about Jesus?") whenever you're

- debriefing a Spirit-dependent experience;

- counseling a teenager who's in crisis;

- responding to false or twisted teachings about Jesus;

- exploring ways to help students tell others about Jesus;

- tackling questions about what Jesus said and did;

- praying for others or for yourself; and

- responding to popular criticisms of Christianity.

The more you ask the question, the more it will become a natural and repetitive habit in every circumstance. We think we know many things about Jesus, but what do we know *for sure*? As a random exercise in asking the Oprah Question, let's read through Matthew 15 quickly, looking for what we know for sure about Jesus as we scan through what he said and did. Ask yourself: "What do I know for sure about Jesus here and here and here?" Let's go...

(Cue elevator music.)

OK, let's compare our lists—here are some samples from mine.

- Jesus likes to answer questions with questions, especially in confrontational situations.

- Jesus isn't afraid to "speak truth to power."

- Jesus is intent on smoking out hypocrisy whenever he smells the stink of it.

- Jesus is more interested in the spirit of the Law than the letter of the Law.

- Jesus is less interested in the words we use to represent who we are than the actions that reveal who we really are.

- Jesus is brutally choosy about the people we follow or allow to influence us.

- Jesus often withdrew from the crowds so he could "re-center" himself.

- Jesus isn't driven by sympathy; he's intent on loving us, not sympathizing with us.

- Jesus is wildly unpredictable.

Now, after this short exercise, get in touch with your own "worship level." I'm more deeply affected by the breadth and depth of who Jesus is, and I can't help myself from wanting to revel in him. Whenever we focus on the red stuff, this is the fruit that results. We're drawn like magnets to Jesus, and we give our soul something solid to feed on. This simple practice—asking the modified Oprah Question about the red stuff—will transform the way your students relate to Jesus.

Here's another simple habit that yields similar results. I call it Jesus Did/Jesus Didn't. I'll give you a taste of how this works. Get a piece of paper and something to write with, then choose a chapter from one of the four Gospels. On your paper, draw a line down the middle to create two columns; label the first column "Jesus Did" and the other "Jesus Didn't." Read through that chapter looking for things Jesus embraced, advised, or did, and list them under the "Jesus Did" column. Then, to spark your thinking even more, go back through that list and brainstorm the opposite of each thing you've listed. For example, if you write, "He healed people of sickness" on the "Jesus Did" side, you can write, "He didn't ignore or leave sick those who came to him seeking healing" on the "Jesus Didn't" side.

Just as the Oprah Question can infiltrate our engagement with students until it becomes like breathing for us, the Jesus Did/Jesus Didn't mentality can grow into a reflexive practice. Whether you use it on a broader scale (as a specific filter for a Bible study) or in a micro way (pausing to ask, "What did Jesus really do here?" and "What didn't Jesus do here?" whenever you're focusing your attention on him), it has real traction when it becomes a way of life, not a mere strategy.

5. Ask Better Questions—Jesus used great questions to teach his followers how to think critically and biblically. My friend Bob Krulish, associate pastor at my church in Denver, once scoured all four Gospels to extract every single question Jesus asked. He ended up with an astonishing 287 questions! And what explosive questions Jesus asked, so potent with "wake up" leverage:

- "Which is easier: to say to the paralytic, 'Your sins are forgiven,' or to say, 'Get up, take your mat and walk?' " (Mark 2:9).

- "Which is lawful on the Sabbath: to do good or to do evil, to save life or to kill?" (Mark 3:4).

- "How can Satan drive out Satan?" (Mark 3:23).

- "Why do you call me good?" (Mark 10:18).

I could go on and on with this list. Jesus literally peppered his followers and religious leaders with critical-thinking questions. And we can do likewise by simply creating and asking good questions until it becomes almost second nature. Let's play with this right now, with a question from a recent Bible study published in Group Magazine: "Why does God instruct believers to regularly remember Jesus' sacrifice on the cross?"

Before I take a whack at improving this question, here's a truth about question-asking: Jesus modeled critical-thinking questions that are surprising, specific, and personal.

- *Surprising* means you include something in the question that catches people off guard.

- *Specific* means you narrow the question from a broad focus to a very narrow focus. Your question should address only one well-defined target. So many bad questions are really two questions in one.

- *Personal* means the question includes something that requires a personal response, not a theoretical response. It requires people to share out of their heart, not just their head.

Now, how can I make my test question better reflect Jesus' standards? I noticed a yellow highlighter sitting on my desk, so I came up with this: "Let's say you open your Bible in the morning and find that God has used his yellow highlighter to mark every place that references Jesus' sacrifice on the cross; why might he do that to your Bible?" Surprising, specific, and personal.

When we ask better questions about Jesus, we create better conversations about him. That's why I've created a question-practice that you can use for any teaching situation in your ministry. It's called the "Three-Question Strategy." You can use this simple-but-dynamic learning strategy whenever you're studying or teaching a Scripture passage that includes things Jesus said and did. First, choose a passage that's rich in "targets"—one packed with examples of Jesus engaging people. Then make three small signs with the following written on them:

1. "What did Jesus really say?" *(Think of the context.)*

2. "What did Jesus really do?" *(What impact did his actions have?)*

3. "How did people really experience Jesus?" *(Look for emotional reactions.)*

Post the three signs in three corners of your meeting area, and put a pile of Bibles under each sign. Then form trios and have them decide which person in their group will go to each of the three corners—then have them split up and go to their assigned corner. Once they get to their corner, they should find a partner, open a Bible to the passage you're exploring, and work together to answer *only* their corner question.

Give students four or five minutes to explore their passage, answer their question, and write their observations. Then ask them to return to their original trio and share what they discovered in their corner discussion. After 5 or 10 minutes, gather everyone together and ask your "essential question": "Who do you say Jesus is?"

6. Practice the Jesus Push-Back—Because false beliefs about Jesus are keeping teenagers from loving him with all their heart, soul, mind, and strength, we must help them learn how to expose and undermine these misconceptions that are "wolves in sheep clothing." We live in a lazy-thinking culture. All of us, students and adults alike, have learned to soak in false "truths" and misleading assumptions about Jesus with little or no push-back. So we train kids to do what Jesus did when Satan tempted him in the wilderness: Every time his enemy threw a lie at him, cloaked as a truth, Jesus pushed back with a biblical truth. And whenever he encountered a "conventional cultural truth" that contradicted the "norms" of the kingdom of God, Jesus pushed back using this repeated refrain: "You have heard it said, but I say...."

Contrary to popular assumptions about followers of Christ, Jesus isn't an anti-intellectual. In fact, he's challenged us to maximize our minds in our pursuit of him and in the way we live our lives for him. Our conventional models for discipleship training—almost always some version of an "information download" seasoned with a video or a story—are fatally flawed, in much the same way our conventional models for public education are fatally flawed. I heard this fatal flaw threaded through an investigative report on why fewer than half of all Colorado students score at grade level in science, and most lose interest in it by fourth grade. Replace "science" with "biblical truth" in public radio reporter Jenny Brundin's report, and the impact is prophetic in scale:

> **Brundin:** When you explore the gargantuan question of why so many kids are failing in science, you find some of the answers just by talking to high school junior Elizabeth Ramsey.

> **Ramsey:** A lot of us did not enjoy science class during middle school, and it kind of carried through with us here. Either they [teachers] just talked at us and we didn't really do anything— or we took the occasional note and listened.

Brundin: So what's going on in classrooms? Lots of talk about facts and procedures. And students mostly just listen. They don't get their hands on things, or they're often not required to figure things out on their own—that's according to a National Research Council study of high school science classrooms. [The key is] getting kids to think critically and invent, using real-world examples. Here's Barry Cartright, former science specialist with the state Department of Education.

Cartright: Recent research has found that the method of delivery isn't as important as making sure the kids are really engaged in the material and having to do some deep thinking about it.

Brundin: That means "minds-on" instead of just "hands-on." They have to be mentally engaged. And that means asking questions, debating ideas, and gathering evidence to refine those ideas. The teacher guides the discussion and discovery. She asks challenging and reflective questions. Students who discover the answers will remember them much better than if a teacher told them in a lecture. Here's teacher Trish Loeblein's advice.

Loeblein: Try to figure out how to get the teacher out of the center stage and how to get the students realizing that they're the learners and that they need to be the doers.[12]

If our goal is for kids to discover the truth about Jesus and what it means to follow him, we'll need to find more ways to help them think critically about the "self-evident truths" they hear repeated over and over in their culture. The practice I call "The Jesus Push-Back" simply uses the framework Jesus has already given us—"You have heard it said...but I say..."—to compare and contrast the common beliefs and conventional wisdoms of our culture. To start, we have to drag commonly accepted "truths" in our culture into the light, then match them with a kingdom-of-God truth that Jesus revealed.

Let's try this with a few sampler "truths" that match up well with a few of the Beatitudes.

YOU HAVE HEARD IT SAID...	BUT I SAY...
• The weak and unsuccessful in life are modern-day lepers; they aren't people we want to hang around.	• "Blessed are the poor in spirit, for theirs is the kingdom of heaven."
• Never let them see you cry.	• "Blessed are those who mourn, for they shall be comforted."
• If you want to succeed in life, you'll need to push your way to the top.	• "Blessed are the meek, for they will inherit the earth."

When teenagers practice this "You have heard it said... but I say..." rhythm often enough, we turn on a switch in them that can't be turned off—ever. They learn to think through a permanent filter we've helped construct for them. It's called "holy skepticism." When they're operating in it, they accept no "conventional truths" that contradict the truths Jesus revealed. They learn to think like him in every circumstance, because they're discovering how countercultural he was in his thinking.

Another simple way to exercise your students' critical-thinking muscle and get them digging deeper into Jesus is to include a regular "Problem Time" segment when you're together. Here's how it works: Develop a list of biblical problems connected to Jesus that need a solution. These are conundrums that we can't make sense of, or things Jesus did that seem counterintuitive, or stuff he said that makes us scratch our head. For example:

- Why did Jesus treat the beggar woman in Matthew 15 so harshly?

- Why, in John 7, did Jesus tell his brothers he wouldn't attend a feast in Judea, then later go anyway?

- Why did Jesus choose to heal a man born blind by spitting in the dirt, making a mud pack, then smearing it on the man's face and forcing him to walk through town to wash in a pool?

- Why did Jesus choose Judas as a disciple?

We could go on and on here. The idea is to identify and list all the "Jesus problems" you can come up with, and then ask your group (in whatever setting you're in) to wrestle with one and come up with some possible solutions. Simply sprinkle these problems into your regular events and activities.

7. Use Parables the Way Jesus Did—A parable is a story that has a truth locked up in it. And that truth will remain locked unless we pay attention to the parable, search for its key, and open it. Jesus speaks in parables because he wants us to experience who he is and what life is like in his "native country"—which the Bible calls the kingdom of God—not just listen to static explanations of him. Just as any sojourner from a foreign land would do, Jesus has humbled himself to "speak our language," but he also wants us to learn what is native to him, and he uses parables to help us.

The difference between telling students principles and truths they should embrace and introducing them to the language of parable is the difference between me merely describing what's in the center of a delicious Reese's Peanut Butter Cup and inviting you to actually bite into one. For example, rather than merely urging us to take risks because risk is native to the kingdom of God, Jesus tells the parable of the talents. He draws us inside a compelling story, then asks us to find the treasure buried there. And that treasure is this: Jesus expects us to reflect his character and personality by taking risks on behalf of him.

There are many creative ways to make the pursuit and experience of parables a staple in your ministry:

- **Pursue Jesus' Parables**—Jesus told so many parables—some tiny and some epic—that we have plenty of possibilities to pursue. In general, his parables can be divided into two basic "species." The first is oriented toward revealing the "norms" of the kingdom of God. The second is focused on revealing the character and personality of God. You can use either species as a launching pad for coming to know Jesus more intimately. Use the first species to ask your students: "What is the kingdom of God like?" Use the second to ask them: "What is God like?" In small groups or all together, choose a parable to pursue, from either category, and then have kids read it and answer the "macro" question attached to it ("What is the kingdom of God like?" or "What is God like?"). Here are a few parables that fit into each category:

THE KINGDOM OF GOD IS LIKE…	GOD IS LIKE…
• Parable of Wheat and Weeds—Matthew 13:24-30 (*God is more concerned about growing wheat than pulling weeds.*)	• Parable of the Great Physician—Matthew 9:10-13 (*He is a healer and inviter of the outsider.*)
• Parable of the Yeast—Matthew 13:33 (*A small addition makes a big difference.*)	• Parable of the Moneylender—Luke 7:40-47 (*He is an appreciator of the desperate and indebted.*)
• Parable of the Treasure in the Field—Matthew 13:44 (*Treasure belongs to those who appreciate it.*)	• Parable of the Lost Sheep—Luke 15:3-7 (*He is a pursuer of lost valuables; and he's a partier.*)

- **Unlocking Parables From Created Things**—Remember the startling truth Paul revealed in Romans 1:20 (NASB): "Since the creation of the world His invisible attributes, His eternal power and divine nature, have been clearly seen, being understood through what has been made." If you have access to God's creation, no matter how minimal the access, you can help your students learn how to extract parable truths from whatever they find. Simply bring in samples (flowers, rocks, pine cones, plants, leaves, whatever), or have kids go outside and find anything from God's creation that they can bring back to your gathering place. Ask them to study their object in silence while asking this question of God: "What does this show me about your 'power, nature, or attributes'?" Then have them wait in silence, while continuing to study their object. Encourage students to "receive" whatever comes to them in this silence. Then end the time of silence by asking them to share their insight with a partner, a small group, or the whole group.

- **Discover Parables Embedded in Cultural Influences**—Pay attention to the songs, TV shows, and films that fill up students' cultural landscape, looking for parables embedded in them. Show your students a movie or TV segment that includes a parable, or have them listen to a song with a parable, and then process the parable through Jesus-centered discussion questions. Some of these cultural snippets are what you might call "low-hanging fruit."

One example is the scene from the film version of C.S. Lewis' *The Lion, the Witch, and the Wardrobe* where Mr. and Mrs. Beaver describe Aslan (Jesus) to Lucy Pevensie, who's visiting Narnia for the first time. Have kids watch the scene, and then ask them: "In the Bible, how was Jesus 'unsafe but good' to the people around him? How has Jesus been 'unsafe but good' in your life?"

Parables just like this one are buried throughout the created entertainment your teenagers are ingesting right now. Not everything in these influences is a parable, of course, but God has shrewdly buried clues about himself in their culture. It's up to us to find them and use them to point kids back to who Jesus really is, and what living in his kingdom is really like. Jesus constantly mined parables from the culture of his day. Remember the parables of the laborers in the field, the weeds and the wheat, and the pearl of great price? Jesus drew these stories directly from his cultural influences. They were very familiar to people he was trying to teach.

- **Create Experiential Parables**—Another way to plunge students more deeply into Jesus' parables is to create experiences that mirror them. The idea is to capture the essence of a parable in a simple experience that plunges kids into *doing*, not merely *hearing*. Here's an example, using the parable of the good shepherd (John 10:1-5). Have your teenagers each find a partner; one person will be the Shepherd, the other will be the Sheep. Give a blindfold of some kind to each of the Sheep and have them put it on. Scatter the Shepherds around the room, each far away from their assigned Sheep. Then ask the blindfolded Sheep to find their way back to their Shepherd by only listening to his or her voice. Here's the catch: Shepherds can only call out "Sheep! Sheep!" to try to guide their Sheep back to them. Give them one minute to do this, and see how many are successful. Then have all the Sheep take their blindfolds off, find their Shepherd (if they haven't already), and discuss these questions: "What made this activity hard for you? What makes it difficult for you in everyday life to recognize Jesus' voice?"

- **Mine Parables From Your Life**—Jesus hasn't only planted parables in his creation, he's also planted them in your life's story. In other words, you've had experiences in your life that have parable-truths locked up in them. The sad truth is that we often fail to unlock those truths from our own lives because we're not paying close attention. Think of a story from your life—anything that surfaces in your mind, or a story that's memorable because it impacted you (positively or negatively).

  (Cue elevator music.)

  Then ask God in the silence: "How might this story be a parable—something that reveals who you are, or what life is like in your kingdom?" What surfaces for you in the quiet? If you wait long enough, the parable-truth will emerge from your story.

For example, I was driving down the highway during rush hour and saw a bunch of papers swirling around, getting chewed up in the traffic. I passed an off-ramp, where I saw a guy getting out of his car to grab the last few sheets of paper stuck on the back of his car. He'd obviously stacked his important papers on his car when he left home, then forgot they were there. So I asked Jesus to show me the "parable connection" in this story. In other words, how can this story teach me something about who God is, or what life in God's kingdom is like? The parable connection Jesus revealed to me has to do with the consequences of my sin. I can be forgiven by him, but like that paper scattered all over the highway, I can't keep the effects of my sin from spreading.

CHAPTER FOUR

Help Students Embrace Their "True Name"

"Hello. My name is Inigo Montoya. You killed my father. Prepare to die." — Mandy Patinkin, in *The Princess Bride*

If you were born a Native American 200 years ago, or a Jew 2,000 years ago, the name you received from your parents wouldn't merely express their sensibilities and preferences; it would project onto you an identity your parents hoped you would live into. Your naming would be less of a label and more of a description; less of a nod to history and more of an act of faith and hope. That's because these cultures understood a truth that we find in the kingdom of God: *The names we embrace in our life are the names we become.*

We're now near the end of this journey, and so far we've exclusively explored practices that target only the first of two Core Questions extracted from Matthew 16: "Who do I say Jesus is?" But the second Core Question—"Who does Jesus say I am?"—is a crucial bookend. After the fisherman Simon "names" Jesus as Messiah, Jesus renames him Peter (*Petros,* which means "rock"). Jesus says, "I also say to you that you are Peter, and upon this rock I will build My church; and the gates of Hades will not overpower it" (Matthew 16:18, NASB).

In renaming his closest friend with a descriptive word that had never before been used as a name, Jesus answers two big questions for him: *Who am I?* and *What am I doing here?* The universal rhythm embedded here is both important and profound. As we name Jesus, he names us. And the name he gives each of us projects onto us an identity born out of his faith in us. In the church we often talk about our faith in God, but we rarely explore the biblical reality that Jesus has faith in *us*. He created in us an identity that's tied to a purpose in his kingdom, and our journey with him through life is a continuous revelation of that identity. He is bent on revealing our true identity that's tied to our true name in the kingdom.

But because the names we embrace are the names we become, our name is the chosen battleground for God's enemy in our life. We're caught in the middle of a war over our identity; in fact, every assault from hell on our life always has a component designed to destroy our God-given identity. If God's enemy can pollute or destroy what is most true about us, then we'll live out of a false identity and fuel his purposes in our life—and his purposes are to "steal, kill, and destroy." This is why it's so crucial for youth ministry leaders to help their students discover, embrace, and live out of their true identity in Christ—their "true name." As we plant a grand pursuit in their lives—"Who do I say Jesus is?—we simultaneously introduce a companion pursuit—"Who does Jesus say I am?"

Has Jesus ever answered this overshadowing question in your life? When have you sensed him revealing to you who you really are? I remember my experience of this so well. It was a little over 10 years ago. I was speaking at a youth ministry conference—the last place I wanted to be at that moment in my life. My wife and I were in the throes of a significant challenge to our young marriage. I'd left for the speaking trip upset and worried; I could sense our relationship was in some danger, and it was killing me. I mean I literally felt like someone was repeatedly jamming a dagger into my gut. I walked through the halls of the convention center hoping no one would recognize me so I wouldn't have to talk with anyone. My interior conversation was full of accusations and criticisms—all directed at myself. My identity was under full-scale assault, and I was sinking fast.

It was during one of my wall-hugging walks down a crowded hallway that I felt God stop me in my tracks. He spoke to me like a lightning bolt. It seemed so clear that I had to step into an empty room and write it all down as the words came gushing at me. I couldn't have been more shocked (and named) by what I sensed. Here's what I wrote down:

> You're a quarterback. You see the field. You're squirming away from the rush to find space to release the ball. You never give up. You have courage in the face of ferocity—in fact, ferocity draws out your courage. You want to score even when the team is too far behind for it to matter. You love the thrill of creating a play in the huddle, under pressure, and spreading the ball around to everyone on the team. You have no greater feeling than throwing the ball hard

to a spot and watching the receiver get to it without breaking stride. In fact, you love it most when the receiver is closely covered and it takes a perfect throw to get it to him. You have the same feeling when you throw a bomb and watch the receiver run under it, or when you tear away from the grasp of a defender, or when you see and feel blood on your elbows or knees and feel alive because of it. You love to score right after the other team has scored, but you want to do it methodically, first down by first down, right down the field. You love fourth down! You want to win, but you're satisfied by fighting well.

Many years after this crisis in my life, Jesus used its brutal leverage in my soul to unveil my true identity and bring radical and beautiful change in my marriage. Of course, "Quarterback" is just a metaphor for something much more pertinent and treasured: the true nature of my heart and identity. God was describing me as I *really* am, and he did it at a desperate moment in my life. Instead of fixing my problem, he revealed my true name. And as the years go by I yield, more and more, to my true identity. In so many ways, youth ministry leaders are the midwives in the birth (or rebirth) of a Jesus-centered identity in the lives of teenagers. Nothing you do in ministry will impact them more deeply or broadly, and it will bear fruit for their rest of their lives.

THE PRACTICE OF POSITIVE LABELING

I know "labeling" is akin to a sin in our culture today, but God is calling us—as mentors and leaders who recruit and train mentors—to vigorously, passionately, positively label our students. Positive Labeling is the key to helping them hear from Jesus about who they really are. The point here isn't simply to become more affirming. Affirmation is designed to make someone feel good about who they are. The practice of Positive Labeling is designed to reveal to a person his or her true nature. The goal is to pay attention to what God is doing in your teenagers, identify it, and name it—to help them hear how Jesus describes them.

When you practice Positive Labeling with your teenagers, you'll learn to act like a detective in their lives—like Sherlock Holmes looking for evidence of their "real name." You'll learn to pay attention to and pounce on little details that reveal a God-given identity in your students. The goal is to solve the mystery of their purpose in God's kingdom—to set the stage for them to hear how God describes their true identity.

I created a simple worksheet to help energize this process. It's called The Sherlock Holmes File (next page). You simply choose a teenager in your group you know pretty well and then answer a few simple questions about that young person.

Try it right now. Plug a teenager's name into the worksheet and take a few minutes to fill it out.

The Sherlock Holmes File

for _____

1. Three things I've noticed that this person seems to love:

*

*

*

2. Three ways I've seen this person contribute:

*

*

*

3. One way I've experienced this person's strength and/or gifting:

4. When this person seems most alive, he/she is usually doing this:

5. One thing this person does that seems to come easily:

6. One way this person could likely serve in ministry:

7. Stop now to pray: "God, who do you say this person is?"
Write what you sense or "hear."

8. Positive Label: On a regular basis, here's how I will
"name" this person—what Jesus has revealed about
him/her:

This is a very powerful process, so don't take it lightly. It's God who knows your teenagers' real names, and it's God who will reveal those names to each of them. In Isaiah 43:1 (NASB) God says: "Do not fear, for I have redeemed you; I have called you by name; you are Mine!" This isn't a process any of us should do alone. Choose people in your ministry who know your teenagers well, and have each person fill out this worksheet for a different kid. If no one knows a teenager well enough to fill out a sheet, that's telling you something. It's time to pursue.

After you fill out these sheets, get together as a group to discuss what you've learned. When you're all doing this regularly and you commit to communicating their "true identity" in a multitude of ways, your students will be encouraged to consciously move toward who they really are and give what they have to give. This skill of Positive Labeling will infuse your mentoring with power.

By the way, before you play with this idea, I suggest you fill out The Sherlock Holmes File for yourself and ask someone close to you to fill it out for you, too. After both of you have filled out the sheet, compare what you've written. Then go to your favorite coffee shop, bakery, or hot wings emporium and discuss these simple questions: *What do we notice about the similarities between our lists; what stands out, and why? What do we notice about the differences between our lists; what stands out, and why?*

ASKING THE QUESTION

In addition to acting like Sherlock Holmes in students'
lives and helping them discover their true, God-given
identity, we can also help them explore the answer to
this life-changing Core Question: "Who does Jesus say
I am?" Find a place to do this where teenagers can have
some quiet space, where they can have a sense of safety
and isolation. Retreats are a great setting to try this
experiment. The key is to do this at a time when your
students are naturally at a lower energy level and to make
sure they have the physical and emotional space they
need to feel "alone."

They'll need something to write on and with. Then, in
the quiet, have them simply ask Jesus: "Who do you say I
am?" Before they ask Jesus this question, instruct them
to do two things: "Tell God you want him to silence your
own voice, and then ask him to silence the voice of his
enemy." Then have students sit quietly and ask Jesus
the question: "Who do you say I am?" Have them write
what they sense—it could be a word, a Scripture passage,
a picture—anything. Assure them they won't have to
share any of this with others unless they want to. Remind
them it's possible they may not hear anything from God
at this time, and that's OK, too. Finally, after they finish
this activity, ask those students who'd like to share about
their experience to do so. Then be available for private,
one-on-one connection times for kids who'd like to

discuss the experience but don't want to do it in front of other teenagers.

Teenagers are longing, like we are, to discover their true identity, and to find out if God cherishes and enjoys them. And we've been invited into that epic mission with them. We, like Jesus our Master, are called to "set captives free," and the primary captivity of God's children is their imprisonment inside a false identity. The names we embrace are the names we become.

◊ ◊ ◊

Jesus-centered youth ministry is a lot like a magnifying glass. When we use Spurgeon's beeline-to-Jesus as the "curved lens" for everything we do, and put it between Jesus and our kids, something flames up. We're lighting a fire in our teenagers, and ourselves. And this particular fire is a "consuming fire," which means we all end up consumed by and for Jesus. That's a nice description of the Christian life in full: following Christ because you're consumed by him, because he's the hub of your wheel, because you're undeniably, unapologetically, aggressively Jesus-centered.

ENDNOTES

[1] Charles Sheldon, *In His Steps* (Uhrichsville, OH: Barbour Publishing, 2005).

[2] Scott Thumma, "A Health Checkup for U.S. Churches" by Hartford Institute for Religion Research (from a presentation at the Future of the Church Summit at Group Publishing, Loveland, Colorado, October 22, 2012).

[3] From the raw footage of videotaped interviews of teenagers across America, in 2005.

[4] To learn more about the *National Study of Youth and Religion,* go to youthandreligion.com or pick up Dr. Christian Smith's book (with Melinda Lundquist Denton) *Soul Searching: The Religious and Spiritual Lives of American Teenagers* (New York, NY: Oxford University Press, 2005).

[5] From a Group Magazine survey of more than 10,000 Christian teenagers attending a Group Workcamp in the summer of 2006.

[6] N.T. Wright, *Following Jesus: Biblical Reflections on Discipleship* (Grand Rapids, MI: Eerdmans, 1994), ix.

[7] From my own transcription of Peter Kreeft's lecture "The Shocking Beauty of Jesus," given at Gordon-Conwell Seminary on September 20, 2007, and later expanded upon in his book *Jesus-Shock* (St. Augustine's Press, 2008).

[8] Brennan Manning, *Ruthless Trust* (New York, NY: Harper Collins Publishers, 2002), 88.

[9] Ned Erickson learned this progression from his ministry partners in Young Life.

[10] spurgeon.us/mind_and_heart/quotes/j.htm

[11] From a post on Twitter by Timothy Keller, on May 22, 2014.

[12] From a Colorado Public Radio report by Jenny Brundin titled "Science in Colorado Classrooms: Big Bang or Black Hole?—Part 1," first aired on October 5, 2012.

Teenagers need to experience more than just a fun event or a good Bible lesson. **They need a real encounter with Jesus.** Guide your entire ministry to a Jesus-centered focus with these innovative resources.

SAVE 25% when you purchase all 4!

SHIFT THE FOCUS OF YOUR MINISTRY

Jesus-Centered Youth Ministry
Moving From Jesus-Plus to Jesus-Only
By Rick Lawrence

DRAW YOUR TEAM CLOSER TO JESUS

Jesus-Centered Youth Ministry: Guide for Volunteers
Moving From Jesus-Plus to Jesus-Only
By Rick Lawrence

REINTRODUCE TEENAGERS TO THE REAL JESUS

Reframing Jesus DVD Curriculum
A Fresh Look Into a Familiar Face
4-Week Small Group Video Curriculum
By Kurt Johnston (with 6 Bonus Training Videos for Leaders by Rick Lawrence)

HELP STUDENTS LIVE A JESUS-CENTERED LIFE

Reframing Jesus Devotional
A Fresh Look Into a Familiar Face
By Rick Lawrence and Kurt Johnston; Illustration by Storm

Purchase this essential kit for your youth ministry at

simplyyouthministry.com